Easter Program Builder No. 31

LILLENAS®
DRAMA

Easter Program Builder No. 31

Compiled by Kim Messer

lillenas
PUBLISHING COMPANY
PO Box 419527
Kansas City, MO 64141

Questions? Please write or call:

Lillenas Publishing Company
Drama Resources
P. O. Box 419527
Kansas City, MO 64141
Phone: 816-931-1900 • Fax: 816-412-8390
E-mail: drama@lillenas.com
Web Site: www.lillenasdrama.com

Cover design: Keith Alexander
Interior design: Sharon Page
Editor: Kimberly Meiste

CONTENTS

Recitations
Preschool 7
Ages 5 to 7 9
Ages 8 to 10 11
Ages 11 to 13 13
Adult Recitations
There's More to Easter 15
Easter, More or Less 16
Readers Theatre
Hosanna! Hosanna! 17
Worship Services
Were You There? 21
Good Friday's Service: There at the Cross 23
Easter Sunday's Service: There at the Empty Tomb 30

RECITATIONS

Preschool

Jesus Said

Jesus said,
"I'll be back from the dead."
Now we
Get to live free!

Ray Ressem

Our Risen Lord

Life He brings.
  New hope and love.
Many *blessings*
  From above.

Dorothy Heibel

Jesus Died for Me

Jesus died for me
So all the world could see
That we can always be
One hundred percent free!

Emma & Kim Messer

Empty Tomb

(Children can hold a sign that says, "It's Easter Day!" and prompt the audience to repeat the phrase with them.)

Empty tomb,
Flowers in bloom,
Everyone say,
"It's Easter Day!"

Ray Ressem

Joys

Easter
  Is a time to sing
Of all the joys
  Our Savior brings!

Dorothy Heibel

Easter Mess

(For a boy with some "pretend" smudge marks on his face and hands. Can be performed with "Easter Dress.")

I tried to look my best
But now I'm an Easter mess.
I ran from the car to the church
And landed in the dirt.
(He holds his hands up.)

Ray Ressem

Easter Dress

(To perform with "Easter Mess." A little sister stands in a pretty dress.)

Brother is a mess
But I have a pretty dress.
I listened to Momma say
Don't run to church that way!
(She smiles and holds her hands in front of her before exiting.)

Ray Ressem

The Cross

The cross that held
My Savior dear
Tells me now
To have no fear.

Ray Ressem

Easter Peace

(Child holding stuffed toy bird or drawing of a dove)

Jesus is gentle
As a dove,
Bringing peace,
New hope and love.

Dorothy Heibel

Pretty Easter Flowers

Pretty Easter flowers
Remind us of His power,
How He came to save
Risen from the grave.

Ray Ressem

It's Easter

Rise and shine
For Easter is here,
Bringing new Hope
For a springtime of cheer.

Dorothy Heibel

What a Friend

(Can be followed with kids' choir and congregation singing "What a Friend We Have in Jesus.")

What a friend
Jesus is to me.
Thank you, Lord.
You've set us free!

Kim Messer

Ages 5 to 7

The Joy of Easter

(A short call to worship for a child)

May you feel the joy of Easter
As we celebrate today.
May we feel Christ's love
Within our hearts
Bringing happiness
All the way!

Dorothy Heibel

Happy Easter

I'm glad it's Easter;
  I'm glad it's spring.
I want to shout
  And I want to sing.
  (To the tune of Happy Birthday*)*
Happy Easter to you;
Happy Easter to you;
Happy Easter, everybody;
Happy Easter to you.
  (Shouting)
Happy Easter!

Margaret Primrose

Easter Time

When Jesus hung upon the cross
  He suffered, our souls to save.
And to those who love and
    believe in Him
  New life and hope He gave.

Dorothy Heibel

Easter Bells

Easter bells ring out
  A message ever new.
Our Risen Lord brings love and
    peace
  To you, and you, and you.
    (Points to audience)

Dorothy Heibel

My Savior and Friend

Jesus is my Savior;
  Jesus is my friend.
Because He died to save me
  My life will never end.

Margaret Primrose

Easter Joy

Easter's the time
To throw off all cares
  And rejoice in the Risen King.
We practice His message
Of forgiveness and love,
  And remember the joy it
    brings.

Dorothy Heibel

An Easter Message

We hear the Easter message—
  Christ has risen from the
    grave.
We know our Lord is ever alive.
  He suffered, our souls to save.

Dorothy Heibel

Easter Song

Easter brings us music.
  Happy voices fill the air.
It's time to end our sadness
  And cast off every care.
For Jesus is our Savior
  And He will ever be
Eternal Ruler of our world,
  Loving Guide to you and me.

Dorothy Heibel

Ages 8 to 10

Jesus Is . . .

(Have children recite, then congregation sing "Jesus Is All the World to Me.")

ALL: Jesus is . . .
CHILD 1: The answer to all our questions.
CHILD 2: The "Yes" to all God's promises.
CHILD 3: The "Amen" to all our prayers.
ALL: Jesus is . . .
CHILD 1: The ultimate example.
CHILD 2: The best of the best.
CHILD 3: The supreme over all.
ALL: Jesus is . . . God's epiphany.
He is everything and all I need.

Kathy Hardee

The Glory of Christ

(Let a child recite this as a benediction.)

May the glory of Christ
Be upon us and those we love.
May we feel His presence with us,
Shining His light from above.

Dorothy Heibel

Easter Acrostic

(Have five children recite, holding up the letter that corresponds with their line. The congregation may then sing "Christ the Lord Is Risen Today.")

CHILD 1: E — Every sin debt, Jesus paid.
CHILD 2: A — All His glory aside was laid.
CHILD 3: S — Sacrifice, the Perfect One.
CHILD 4: T — Truly, He is God's own Son.
CHILD 5: E — Everlasting life He brings.
ALL: R — Risen Savior, King of Kings.

Kathy Hardee

A Reason to Live

(Have children recite, then congregation sing "We All Are One in Mission.")

CHILD 1: The reason I live
Is easy to see.
CHILD 2: I gave all I have
Because Christ died for me.
CHILD 3: I walk in His presence.
I stand in His grace.
CHILD 4: I work with my Savior.
I serve in His place.
CHILD 5: We share in one mission.
We strive for one goal—
ALL: To bring one to Jesus;
To rescue one soul.

Kathy Hardee

Ages 11 to 13

At the Cross

(Recite, then have congregation sing "The Old Rugged Cross.")

Stripes of anguish Jesus bore.
A crown of shame our Savior
wore.
Clothed in horror, grief, and
pain,
He put on sin's ugly stain.
Innocence—nailed to the tree,
To save a sinner just like me.

Kathy Hardee

ADULT RECITATIONS

There's More to Easter

by Elaine Hardt

Easter bunnies and eggs a tradition,
  A token visit to church mere cliché;
Families shopping in preparation
  For just another busy holiday.

Remember Passover, the slaves set free,
  The blood of a lamb placed on their door;
Obedience to God was freedom's key,
  Let the Scriptures tell you more.

Messiah Jesus, Lamb of God, was slain,
  Innocent, redeeming us from sin;
Death could not hold Him, He rose again,
  To receive Him begins new life within.

Some celebrate Easter in lesser ways,
  Let your heart find the deeper reason;
For God's great love let us give Him praise,
  Embrace Him in this holy season.

Easter, More or Less

by Elaine Hardt

The calendar says it, the stores display it,
Greeting cards announce it,
Easter, more or less.

Colored eggs and candy galore;
Spring has sprung in every store.
Family togetherness around the table;
Eat as much as you are able.
It's Easter, more or less.

Across the land the church bells ring,
Preachers preach, great choirs sing;
Choose your level of celebration,
Christian or nonbeliever in participation,
It's Easter, more or less.

God made provision, will we believe?
His Son as Savior, will we receive?
He showed the way in the Passover meal;
Ritual could rob meaning, and blessing, steal.
We're talking about Easter, more or less.

Will I get more of the truth, or will I have less?
God wants me to trust Him so He can bless.
I choose a relationship with Jesus in my heart;
Resurrection Day is my brand-new start.
Instead of some secular Easter.

God said it, His Word announced it,
Take it or leave it,
Easter, more or less.

READERS THEATRE

Hosanna! Hosanna!

A Palm Sunday Reading

by Gordon Williams

Scripture References: Psalm 2:7-9, 118:26; Habakkuk 2:11; Zechariah 9:9; Luke 19:28-40; John 12:12-17 (Unless otherwise noted, all verses are taken from the NKJV.)

VOICE 1: I will declare the decree
The LORD has said to Me:
"You are My Son,
Today I have begotten You."

CHORUS *(in a whisper):* Hosanna! Hosanna!

VOICE 1: Ask of Me, and I will give You
The nations for Your inheritance,
And the ends of the earth for Your possession.

CHORUS *(a little louder):* Hosanna! Hosanna!

VOICE 1: You shall break them with a rod of iron;
You shall dash them to pieces like a potter's vessel.

CHORUS *(full voice):* Hosanna! Hosanna!

VOICE 2: Blessed is he who comes in the name of the LORD!

VOICE 3: Rejoice greatly, O daughter of Zion!
Shout, O daughter of Jerusalem!

VOICE 4: Behold, your King is coming to you;
He is just, and having salvation.

VOICE 5: Lowly, riding a donkey.

VOICE 2: A colt, the foal of a donkey. (TEV)

VOICE 3: A young pack animal. (GWT)

CHORUS: Hosanna to the Son of David! (GWT)

VOICE 4: Now when they drew near to Jerusalem, (Jesus) sent two of His disciples , and He said to them,

VOICE 1: "Go into the village opposite you, and as soon as you have entered it you will find a colt tied, on which no one has sat."

VOICE 2: "A tethered colt." (NJB)

VOICE 3: "One that has never yet been ridden." (TM)

VOICE 4: "Which no man has ever yet sat." (AMP.)

VOICE 1: "Untie it and bring it here."

CHORUS: "A donkey's colt!" (TLB)

VOICE 1: "And if anyone says to you 'Why are you doing this?' say, 'The Lord has need of it,' and immediately he will send it there."

CHORUS: Behold, your King is coming!

VOICE 5: So they went their way, and found the colt tied by the door outside on the street, and they loosed it.

CHORUS: Your King is coming to you! (TEV)

VOICE 2: But some of those who stood there said to them, "What are you doing, loosing the colt?"

VOICE 3: And they spoke to them just as Jesus had commanded.

VOICE 4: "The Lord needs it and will send it back here shortly."

VOICE 3: So they let them go.

VOICE 2: Then they brought the colt to Jesus and threw their clothes on it, and He sat on it.

CHORUS *(whispering):* A colt . . . which no one has ever ridden.

VOICE 3: And many spread their clothes on the road, and others cut down palm branches from the trees and spread them on the road.

VOICE 4: Then those who went before and those who followed cried out, saying:

CHORUS: "Hosanna! Hosanna!"

VOICE 5: "Blessed is He who comes in the name of the Lord!"

CHORUS: "Praise God!" (TEV)

VOICE 2: "Hosanna to the Son of David!" (NRSV)

VOICE 3: "Peace in heaven and glory to God!" (TEV)

VOICE 4: But some of the Pharisees among the crowd said, "Sir, rebuke your followers for saying things like that!" (TLB)

VOICE 5: "Teacher, get your disciples under control!" (TM)

VOICE 2: "Teacher, command your disciples to be quiet!" (TEV)

VOICE 3: "Master, reprimand your disciples!" (NEB)

CHORUS: "Teacher, rebuke your disciples!" (NIV)

VOICE 4: But He answered and said to them,

VOICE 1: "I tell you that if these would keep silent, the stones would immediately cry out."

VOICE 2: "The stones along the road will burst into cheers!" (TLB)

VOICE 3: "The stones will shout aloud." (NEB)

VOICE 4: For in the book of Habakkuk it is written, "For the stone will cry out from the wall, and the beam from the timbers will answer it."

CHORUS: "Hosanna to the Son of David! Blessed is the one who comes in the name of the Lord! Hosanna in the highest heaven!" (NRSV)

VOICE 5: His disciples did not understand these things at first; but when Jesus was glorified, then they remembered that these things were written about Him and that they had done these things to Him.

WORSHIP SERVICES

Were You There?

By L. Ruth Carter

Running Time:

Good Friday Service, approximately 35 to 40 minutes
Easter Sunday Service, approximately 45 to 50 minutes

Theme: This worship service of music, drama, and litany was developed around the Negro Spiritual, "Were You There When They Crucified My Lord?" It is a program in two parts: Good Friday and Easter Sunday. As it asks us the question, "Were you there?" it highlights that God was there and that the events of Calvary and the empty tomb were because of His love for us. Stanzas of the hymn "Were You There?" precede the dramatic monologues. The hymn may be sung by the choir or the congregation. Most of the other songs are suggestions only and may be substituted by any pieces compatible with the theme. Litanies and poetic readings round out the programs.

Cast:

PASTOR
LEADER—To lead litany; could be the pastor
ACTORS—Men and women featured in the monologues
- JOANNA—Wife of Cleopas, a steward in the palace of Pontius Pilate
- PETER—Disciple who failed an important test
- CENTURION—Roman soldier who wondered
- THE OTHER MARY—Mother of James
- SALOME—Mother of John and James
- JOSEPH OF ARIMATHEA—Man who stepped up when it counted

ENSEMBLE—Choir or worship team; any grouping of people to sing "Were You There When They Crucified My Lord?"

Costumes:

JOANNA—A long dark-colored skirt and blouse or dress, with a dark shawl to drape over the head

PETER—Fisherman's clothes (plaid shirt and blue jeans); to give a sense of period, wear a sleeveless, homespun robe over these

CENTURION—A tunic with a wide belt over slacks and shirt

THE OTHER MARY—A long skirt or dress with a shawl for the head; colors should be bright and vibrant

SALOME—Similar to Joanna's, though less "rich"

JOSEPH OF ARIMATHEA—Suit and tie with prayer shawl and yarmulke

Props and Decor:

For Good Friday—

A wooden cross (as close to the actual size as possible)

Three or four hammers on the platform

A box of nails

A bulletin with the litany and songs for each person

Red ribbons, 8 to 12 inches long (One for each person. Optional: inscribe on the ribbons, "My sin—His forgiveness.") Hand them out with the bulletin.

For Easter Sunday—

The wooden cross from Friday's service, now lying down—not flat—decorated with lilies

Lots of light and flowers

Significant space on platform for drama presentation

Production Notes:

There should be a big contrast between the Good Friday and Easter Sunday services. Good Friday should be kept somber and quiet. If possible, have it dark in the sanctuary and encourage the people to go in and sit quietly. Do most of the speaking from the body of the congregation.

Easter Sunday's service is in great contrast to Good Friday's. It should be filled with brightness and energy. Have lots of flowers and the people singing and leading may be much more visible than they were on Good Friday. If people want to chat and visit in the sanctuary before the service begins, great!

While this program is designed for two services, the material provided may certainly be used outside of this format for one service that covers both the Passion and the Resurrection.

Good Friday's Service

There at the Cross

Optional Choral Prelude: Music that highlights the Passion of Jesus Christ.

Call to Worship: John 3:16 NIV

Opening Hymn: "O How He Loves You and Me"[1] (stanza 1)

Welcome

Poem: "God Was There"

God was there. God is love.
    From the beginning, He was there.
        Love was there.
    In love
    He made the world and filled it with every good thing.
    In love
    He made man and woman and breathed His Spirit into
        them.
    He made us so He could love us.
    He made us so we could be His friends.
    He made us and gave us paradise.
    All He wanted from us was our love
    —our love for the world He made
    —our love for each other
    —our love for Him.
    That's all He wanted
    —a love that would fill us and give us all we could ever
        need or want.
    He wanted a love we could freely give.
    He wanted a love we chose to give.
        He gave us the choice. Here is paradise. It is yours.
        Today,
            and today,
                and today,
                    and forever.
I am here.
    Everything here is yours.
        Yours to enjoy.

Yours to take care of.
The fruit is yours.
Yours to eat.
You may eat it all.
All the fruit except one.
Eat that fruit and die.
Such a simple choice. A choice of love.
Without love there would be no choice.
Without choice there would be no love.
We chose the fruit and paradise died.
God grieved.
He was there and He was love.
He promised a way.
Love promised a way.
Love promised a way to pay the price.
Love promised a way to defeat death.
Love promised a Savior.
For centuries God loved us,
worked with us,
showed us the way.
For centuries He showed us
that the spilled blood of a spotless lamb could pay the price for our sin.
For centuries He spoke to us through His prophets.
One day, He said, He would send the final sacrifice—the Lamb of God.
For centuries we did not listen
and the prophets cried out,
"Doesn't anyone believe our report?"

Litany: The Suffering Servant (a paraphrase of Isaiah 53)

LEADER: Doesn't anyone believe us? Hasn't anyone seen God's miraculous power in action? God's servant grew. Like a sapling or a seed that takes root in dry ground, He grew up obeying God.

WOMEN: He wasn't handsome. He was not majestic. There was nothing in His looks that made Him attractive to us.

MEN: He was hated. He was rejected.

WOMEN: He was a man of sorrows, filled with grief.

MEN: No one would look at Him.

WOMEN: We turned our backs on Him.

ALL: We despised Him and said, "He is a nobody!"

LEADER: It was our sorrow He endured, our weaknesses He bore. But we thought He deserved it. We thought God was punishing Him.

MEN: He was wounded and crushed because of our sins.

WOMEN: He was beaten to give us peace.

MEN: He was whipped and made us well.

WOMEN: Completely well.

ALL: We were all like sheep that had wandered off. We each went our own way—did our own thing.

MEN: We were the ones that deserved punishment, not Him. He took our punishment.

WOMEN: He was harshly abused, but He never complained.

MEN: He was silent. As silent as a lamb being led to the slaughter, like a sheep being shorn.

WOMEN: He was condemned to death without a fair trial.

LEADER: Who among us could know what He was doing?

ALL: Who could know He was taking our punishment?

WOMEN: He wasn't dishonest.

MEN: He wasn't violent.

ALL: He never did any wrong, but He was buried like a criminal. He was put in a rich man's tomb.

LEADER: But it was God's plan to crush Him, fill Him with grief. He had to be a sacrifice to take away the sin and guilt of others.

ALL: He was there. He did everything just as God planned.

LEADER: When He sees the good work that is done because of His anguish, He will be content. He is blessed because by His work many may be counted righteous.

ALL: He was there. He did everything just as God planned.

PASTOR: God was there.

Song and Drama: "Were You There?"

Song *(to be sung either by the congregation or an ensemble):*
Were you there when they crucified my Lord?
Were you there when they crucified my Lord?
O — sometimes it causes me to tremble, tremble, tremble.
Were you there when they crucified my Lord?

LEADER: Were you there when they crucified my Lord?

JOANNA *(coming from audience):* I was there. I was there with His mother and some of the other women. When we heard He'd been arrested, we went at once.

I couldn't believe it. How could this be? Only five days before He had ridden into the city on a donkey while the people waved palm branches and shouted, "Hosanna to the King!" I was so glad. At least, I thought, they know who He is. "Hosanna!" they sang. "Hosanna! Save us! He is King!"

But the people—where were they now, the ones who called Him King? Where were they? Were they with the mob that screamed those words, "Crucify Him! Crucify Him!"? How those words pierced me! They thundered into my soul, crushing my spirit.

I followed with His mother and the other women as the soldiers took Jesus up to the place of execution. The Place of the Skull, we call it—out there, next to the garbage dump. He'd come out of the palace His back shredded from the lash of the whip, blood still oozing from countless wounds, a circle of vicious thorns crammed on His head. Oh, the indignity! The outrage! As they marched Him through the city streets, people mocked Him, spat on Him. Others turned their backs on Him. He, who had healed their sick, fed their hungry, and raised their dead. They scorned and derided Him. Such love He had for them and they reviled Him. Yes, I was there when they crucified my Lord. I was there.

PETER *(coming from audience):* Well, I wasn't there. Oh, I'd been there earlier. At supper—the Passover supper—He'd been so strange. "This is My body," He'd said as He tore the bread. "This is My body, broken for you. This is My blood. This is My body." So strange. I didn't understand it. Now all I can think of is His broken body, His spilled blood.

I was there in the garden. I tried to stay awake. I really

did. Once, His deep groaning disturbed me and I sat up. "Father," He prayed, "take this cup of suffering away from Me." His sweat looked like great drops of blood. I couldn't watch. I heard Him say, "But don't do what I want, Father. Do Your will." I fell asleep. We all did. "Can't you stay awake?" Jesus asked us. "Get up and pray, or else temptation will be too much for you." I tried. I failed. And the temptation was too much. When Judas—Judas! One of us! When Judas betrayed Him with a kiss, I was there. When the high priest's soldiers arrested Him and took Him away, I was there. But when they tried Him, when they convicted Him and sentenced Him to death, I was not there. No, I wasn't there. I even—to my shame—denied knowing Him. Was I there when they crucified my Lord? No. No, I wasn't there. I was too scared. I wasn't there. I wasn't there.

Song: Were you there when they nailed Him to the tree?

LEADER: Were you there?

CENTURION *(coming from audience):* I was there. I was there when they nailed Him to the tree. Oh yes, I was there. My hands held the hammer.

I had presided over many executions. You get used to it. Some of us harden ourselves, some even take a sadistic delight in the suffering of the criminals we crucify. They throw out crude insults and gamble for their clothes. Me, I always tried to distance myself from it all, or it would become a corrosive acid, eating away at the very essence of who I was.

This man—this Jesus of Nazareth—was so different from any of the others we'd taken up there. He did not plead or beg. He didn't proclaim His innocence. He didn't curse. I had known His reputation. I had met some people whose lives He'd touched. He'd even healed the servant of one of my fellow officers. He had done no one harm, but here He was. It wasn't my job to question. It was my job to execute orders. So I did. I executed. Without question.

But He was so different! "Forgive them, Father," He said. "Forgive them! They don't know what they're doing." How He found breath to speak, I don't know. His weight on His arms caused His chest to collapse, cutting off His air. He had to push up on His legs in order to speak. Every time He said something, He would push up, His raw, bleeding back scraping against the rough bark of the tree. He said several more things. He asked one of the men there to look after His mother. He spoke to the two thieves hanging next to Him. He was thirsty. They always are—a raging thirst that often turns them into mad men.

His anguish exceeded His physical torment. "My God!" He cried out. "My God, why have You abandoned Me?" Never have I heard such despair, such overwhelming agony. Never. I would have broken His legs to hasten His death, but He gasped out, "It is finished," and died. I know He died. I thrust my spear into His side to make sure. When water mixed with blood gushed out, I knew He was dead.

I knew He was dead. And I wondered. I wondered. Was He more than a man? Was He more than an innocent man? Was He—was He the very Son of God?

I was there. I was there when they nailed Him to the tree.

Ceremony: Being There

PASTOR: Were you there when they crucified my Lord?

This morning, we invite you to be there at the cross. You were handed a ribbon with your bulletin when you came in. The ribbon represents your sins, your bad choices, all those things which keep you from knowing God, which keep you from the friendship He dearly wants with you. Look at the ribbon. Feel it. Think about the sacrifice Jesus made for you. Think of something that keeps you from enjoying a full walk with Jesus. Let the ribbon represent that. Bring it to the cross and nail it there, for it was our sins that nailed Jesus to the cross 2,000 years ago.

Leave the ribbon there, for as it was our sins that nailed Jesus to the cross, it was Jesus who took those sins and removed them from us, as far as the east is from the west.

(PASTOR *nails his ribbon to the cross. The congregation follows suit. Have people sprinkled throughout the sanctuary who know ahead of time so they can set an example. Do not have music playing. The only sounds will be the footsteps of the people and the hammering of the nails. Once everybody has come who is going to come, have a person assigned to stand the cross up.)*

PASTOR *(when cross is standing):* Were you there when they nailed Him to the tree?

Song: "Behold the Lamb"[2]

(Song may be sung a capella, possibly from the back of the church by an ensemble or soloist. Elements should flow seamlessly from one to the other.)

PASTOR: Were you there? Were you there when the sun refused to shine?

Drama: "Were You There?"

Song: Were you there when the sun refused to shine?

LEADER: Were you there? Were you there when the sun refused to shine?

PETER: The sky turned black. The earth shook.

JOANNA: All nature trembled.

CENTURION: "It is finished," He said, and He died.

JOANNA: The sun refused to shine.

(Option: The above four lines may all be spoken by JOANNA.*)*

Hymn Reprise: "O How He Loves You and Me"[3] (stanzas 1 and 2)

Pastor's Remarks

Closing Hymn: "Beneath the Cross of Jesus"[4]

Easter Sunday's Service

There at the Empty Tomb

Optional Choral Prelude: Music that highlights the Resurrection and glory of Jesus Christ.

Opening Hymn: "Christ the Lord Is Risen Today"[5]

Call to Worship: John 3:16

Hymn: "O How He Loves You and Me"[6] (stanza 1)

PASTOR: He is risen!

ALL: He is risen indeed!

Welcome and Opening Prayer

Praise and Worship: More music that highlights the Resurrection—this can be a time of congregational singing, choir and/or special numbers.

Drama: "Were You There?"

THE OTHER MARY *(coming from audience):* I was there! What an amazing, amazing day. I felt like my heart would leap from my breast. I had to leap and dance. I had to shout it. "Jesus is alive!" What a wondrous truth was this? Jesus is alive! And I was there!

I was there when they killed Him. The earth shook, the sun stopped shining. A crushing loneliness engulfed me. He was gone. I knew He was dead. I was there. I watched Him die. I watched Him die and I could do nothing.

All I could do was buy the spices to anoint His body.

We couldn't do it the next day because it was the Sabbath. So we went early Sunday morning. I remember how brightly the sun shone as Joanna, Salome, Mary Magdalene, and I made our way to the garden. It mocked our grief, exposed our anguish to a cold, unfeeling world. I remember, early as it was, how the merchants were already setting up their stalls for the day's business. I remember dogs barking in the distance. I remember children running, intent on some game. I remember a Pharisee picking up his robes as he walked by, to avoid contact with any dirt. I remember a woman bumping into me and spilling water from the jug she carried. I remember thinking, don't they realize what has happened? Don't they realize that something died on Friday? Don't they realize that hope died? That laughter, joy, and love died? Don't they realize that Jesus died?

When we got to the tomb, we found that the stone had been rolled away. We were puzzled, as we had not yet asked anyone to help us with it. We went inside and found it empty. We looked at each other. What was going on? We went back outside. Maybe we had the wrong tomb. But no, this was it. We stepped inside again, giving our eyes a chance to adapt to the dimness. The body of Jesus was not there. We did not know what to do. What had happened to it?

Suddenly the darkness vanished as radiance filled the tomb. Two men, clothed in dazzling robes appeared before us. We were terrified and bowed low before them.

"This is a graveyard," they said. "Why are you looking for the living among the dead?"

We looked at each other. What could they mean?

"Jesus isn't here!" they said. "He has risen from the dead."

But we didn't understand. We were still deeply shocked and grieving. What they were saying was beyond belief.

"Listen." They spoke to us so gently. "Remember, He told you about this back in Galilee. He told you that He would be betrayed by a friend. He told you how He would be given into the hands of sinful men and be crucified. Remember?"

Yes, we remembered.

"That's what happened, isn't it?" they asked.

We nodded, too overcome to speak.

"Don't you remember that He also said He would rise again on the third day?"

We remembered! Yes, we remembered! We remembered and we believed.

We turned and looked at the two men—angels, they were—and they were smiling with a joy that blinded us. We remembered. He would rise again on the third day! This was the third day! He was alive!

I am not a young woman, but I ran. How I ran! We all did. We ran and found the apostles and told them. We told everyone we could. Jesus was alive! Of course, they didn't believe us at first. How could they? We were too excited to be coherent, and when they figured out what we were saying, it was too incredible to be believed. But it was true! He was alive! Soon, they too, believed. And over the next few days, Jesus appeared to many of us, so gloriously alive, so heart-stoppingly real.

(If the actress can sing, insert a solo here: "I Believe in Jesus," by Marc Nelson.)

You ask, was I there? Yes, yes, yes, I was there! Hallelujah! I was there and He was there, standing in our midst! Yes, I was there!

Litany: We Were There (a paraphrase and adaptation of Romans 6:3-10)

LEADER: Were you there? Please turn to the litany that is printed in the bulletin. *(Written text begins)* Were you there when they crucified my Lord?

ALL: We were there.

WOMEN: Don't forget that when we became Christians

MEN: and were baptized to become one with Christ Jesus,

ALL: we died with Him. We were there.

LEADER: Were you there when they nailed Him to the tree?

ALL: We were there.

MEN: We died with Christ by baptism. We were there.

WOMEN: We were buried with Him by baptism. We were there.

MEN: And just as the Father raised Jesus from the dead

WOMEN: by His glorious power,

ALL: now we may live new lives too.

LEADER: Were you there when they laid Him in the tomb?

ALL: We were there.

MEN: Just as we have been united with Jesus in His death, like Him we will be raised to life.

WOMEN: When Jesus died, our old selves, our sinful selves, were crucified with Him, so that sin will no longer have power in our lives.

ALL: We are no longer slaves to sin.

MEN: For when we died with Christ, we were freed from sin's power.

WOMEN: And since we died with Christ, we know we will share His new life too.

LEADER: Were you there when He rose up from the dead?

MEN: We were there.

WOMEN: We were there.

ALL: We were there.

MEN: We are sure of this: Christ rose from the dead. He will never die again. Never.

ALL: Death will never have any power over Him.

WOMEN: He died once to defeat sin. Now He lives for the glory of God!

MEN: Now He lives for the glory of God!

ALL: Now He lives for the glory of God!

LEADER: Were you there?

WOMEN: I was there.

MEN: I was there.

ALL: We were there.

LEADER: Are you here?

WOMEN: I am here.

MEN: I am here.

ALL: We are here.

PASTOR: He is risen!

ALL: He is risen indeed!

PASTOR: He is here!

ALL: He is here indeed!

Special Music: "The Easter Song"[7]

Pastor: He is risen!

ALL: He is risen indeed!

Offering

Poetic Reading: "Resurrection Joy"

(Poem may be sung to Beethoven's "Ode to Joy.")

Alleluia! Alleluia!
Christ is risen from the dead!
Shout our praises! Sing with gladness!
He is risen as He said!
Bend our knees in adoration;
Lift our hands with loud amens.
Alleluia! Alleluia!
To our Savior, Lord and Friend.

Alleluia! Alleluia!
Sing to Christ, God's blessed Son!
Shout our praises! Sing with gladness!
Christ has conquered, Christ has won!
Join our hearts in exultation,
Raise our voices, lift our heads.
Alleluia! Alleluia!
Christ is risen from the dead!

Alleluia! Alleluia!
Glory to our God and King!
Shout our praises! Sing with gladness!
Joyous hearts are caroling.
Christ our Savior bought our pardon,
Paid the price and took our sin.
Alleluia! Alleluia!
Christ is risen from the dead!
Shout our praises! Sing with gladness!
He is risen as He said!

Pastor's Remarks and Prayer

PASTOR: He is risen!

ALL: He is risen indeed!

Closing Chorus: "He Is Lord"[8]

Optional Monologues

If you do not have the cast to do all the monologues as written, you may substitute them with one woman, who will play SALOME.

She will do JOANNA's monologue for stanza one, as well as the last four lines answering stanza three. *(She may also do* THE OTHER MARY *monologue for the Easter service.)* Delete the PETER monologue and replace the CENTURION's with the following:

Song: Were you there when they nailed Him to the tree?

SALOME *(coming from audience):* Every blow of the hammer pounded my heart. The other two—the thieves who were executed with Him—cursed and shrieked out. But Jesus, Jesus did not beg or plead. His thoughts, His heart—even as He endured such soul-destroying anguish—His thoughts were for others. They were for His mother. "Look after her," He told John. They were for the thief who defended Him. "You'll be in paradise with me today," Jesus assured him. They were . . . oh, my Lord! He had mercy even for His tormentors! "Forgive them, Father," He said, even as the pain racked His body and He fought for every breath. "Forgive them. They don't know what they are doing."

What kind of love was this?

Oh, He said He was thirsty. Yes, that. But it wasn't until the very end when the true nature of His agony burst out. "My God," He cried, and His pain tore through my own heart. "My God, why have You forsaken Me?" This was a despair that went far, far beyond the torture of His poor body.

I was there when they nailed Him to the tree.

The following monologue for Joseph of Arimathea may be used if you choose not to include "The Ceremony of the Cross" portion of the Good Friday service. It will replace the ceremony as well as stanza three and the four lines accompanying it.

CENTURION *(see monologue answering "Were you there when they nailed Him to the tree?")*

LEADER: Were you there?

Song: "Behold the Lamb"[9]

LEADER: Were you there when they laid Him in the tomb?

Song: Were you there when they laid Him in the tomb?

JOSEPH OF ARIMATHEA *(coming from audience):* I was there. I had been a secret follower of Jesus. As a member of the Sanhedrin, I had been afraid of what the other Pharisees would do if they knew I trusted Jesus. When my fellow Pharisees attacked Him with trick questions, I stayed quiet. When they schemed and grumbled about Him, I removed myself from them, but said nothing. To publicly align myself with Jesus would cost me my position—something I did not, at the time, think I could sacrifice.

I had so longed for the Kingdom of David to be reestablished in Israel. I knew Jesus was the King—I knew He was the Messiah. My colleagues, however, enjoyed their present status too much to willingly accept a Messiah. They were hostile towards the carpenter from Nazareth, who boldly stood up to their ambitions and hypocrisy. There was only one other member of the Sanhedrin who thought as I did—Nicodemus—and he too stayed quiet about his beliefs. When the high priest's soldiers brought Jesus before our council, neither of us was present. I wonder—would we have spoken out in His defense if we had been there?

The trial was a mockery—hastily fashioned out of lies, fear, and treachery. It was an illegal travesty of justice, but the elders were too incensed to wait. They quickly denounced Him. They had been jealous of His popularity, suspicious of His motives, skeptical about His miracles. They accused Him of defiling our law, the law of Moses, and took Him to the Roman governor for sentencing. Jesus! As pure and spotless as the Passover lamb, He was convicted as a dangerous criminal.

Nicodemus and I were powerless. We could not stop the council. We could not stop the Romans. But we knew it was time to step out and declare ourselves. We could no longer remain silent. To do so would be a betrayal of all that He had done, all that He was. When Jesus died, I went to the governor and asked for His body. I took that wasted, beaten, lacerated body down from the cross and wrapped it in a long linen cloth. Then I put Him in the tomb—my own tomb, which I had recently purchased and had carved out of rock.

Was I there when they put Him in the tomb? Oh, yes. I was there. It took me a while, but finally, finally, I was there.

Additional Notes

All the individual elements of these programs may be used singly within other programs or combined into one program encompassing both the Passion and the Resurrection.

The monologues are designed to be produced simply. The cast may sit in the congregation in order to give the audience a sense of immediacy—to help them feel they are "there." The actors, dressed in street clothes, come from their seats at the appropriate time. They may have a shawl, drape or robe that can be quickly thrown on as they move to the front. The costume extras should not be on display until the actors make their entrances.

Songwriter Credits

1. Kurt Kaiser
2. Dottie Rambo
3. Kurt Kaiser
4. Elizabeth C. Clephane, Frederick C. Maker
5. Charles Wesley
6. Kurt Kaiser
7. Annie Herring
8. Unknown
9. Dottie Rambo